```
THIS BOOK
BELONGS TO:

_____

_____
```

Introduction

Keeping a journal can be a powerful way to work through the strongest emotions.

Psychologists have researched the healing powers of expressive writing, describing it as a way to have an honest and open conversation with yourself and, as the best expert on your own feelings, writing a regular journal allows you the time to express and understand what you are feeling.

Grief is one of the most powerful emotions we experience as humans, and it can be very difficult to discuss a loss with others. Writing is a tried and trusted method for helping people come to terms with the intense, sometimes overwhelming, sorrow they feel at the death of a loved one or loss of something important to you.

So, I commend you for taking the step in this journey toward healing and remember that you are writing only for yourself. You will not be judged, and this is a safe place to express yourself and write out everything that is on your mind and heart.

Like you, so many others have taken this journey and have found healing though with the process outlined in this journal. Take your time and give yourself a break and allow the process to take its course.

Grief is a very personal experience, and a grief journal is a way to express feelings honestly.

My hope and prayer is that this journal will give you the healing that you are looking for and deserve.

Warmest regards,

Geno Ryan

LIST OF EMOTIONS PT. 1

absorbed
acceptance
aching
admiration
adventurous
adoration
admiration
adrift
adulation
affection
afraid
affection
aggravation
aggressive
agitation
agony
agreeable
alarm
alone
aloof
alert
alienation
alive
amazement
amusement
anger
angst
animated
anguish
annoyance
anticipation
antsy
anxiety
apologetic
appalled

apprehension
aroused
ashamed
assertive
assured
astonishment
attachment
attracted
attraction awe
awkward

baffled
betrayed
bitterness
blessed
bliss
blue
bold
boredom
bitter
brave
bubbly

calculating
calm
capricious
caring
cautious
charmed
cheerful
closeness
cocky
cold
comfortable

compassion
complacent
compliant
composed
conceited
concerned
confident
contempt
content
contentment
cowardly
crabby
crazed
crazy
cross
cruel

daring
defeated
defiance
delighted
denial
dependence
depressed desire
detached
disappointment
disapproval
discontent
disenchanted
disgust
disillusioned
dislike
dismay
distant

distressed
dismissed
displeasure
dissatisfied
distraction
distress
disturbed
doom
dread

eager
earnest easy-
going ecstasy
ecstatic
edgy
elation
embarrassment
emotion
emotional
empty
enamored
enchanted
enjoyment
enraged
enraptured
enthralled
enthusiasm
envious
envy
equanimity
euphoria
exasperation
excited
exhausted

extroverted
exuberant

fascinated
fatalistic
fear
fearful
ferocity
flummoxed
flustered
fondness
frazzled
fretful
fright
frightened
frustration
furious
fury

generous
glad
gloating
gloomy
glum
greedy
grief
grim
groggy
grouchy
grumpy
guarded
guilt

happiness
happy

LIST OF EMOTIONS PT. 2

harried
hesitant
hollow
homesick
hopeless
horrified
hostility
humiliation
hurt
hysteria

infatuated
insecurity
insulted
interested
introverted
irritation
isolation

jaded
jealous
jittery
jolliness
jolly
joviality
joy
jubilation
jumpy

keen
kind
kind hearted
kindly

Laid Back

Lazy
Like
loathing
loneliness
lonely
longing
love
lulled
lust

mad
merry
misery
modesty
mortificatio

naughty
neediness
neglected
nervous
nirvana

open
optimism
ornery
outgoing
outrage

panic
paralyzed
paranoid
passion
Passive
Peaceful
Pensive

pessimism
petrified
pity
placid
pleased pride
proud
pushy

quarrelsome
queasy
querulous
quick-witted
quiet
quirky

rage
rapture
rejection
relief
relieved
remorse
repentance
resentment
resigned
restless
revulsion
roused

sad
sadness
sarcastic
sardonic
satisfaction
scared

scorn
self-assured
self-congratulatory
self-satisfied
sentimentality
serenity
shame
shaken
shock
skeptical
smug
sorrow
sour
sorry
spellbound
spite
startled
stingy
stoical
stressed
subdued
submission
suffering
surprise
sympathy

tenderness
tense
terror
threatening
thrill
timidity
torment
tranquil
trepidation

triumphant
trust
twitchy

uncomfortable
unhappiness
unhappy
upset
uptight

vain
vanity
venal
vengeful
vexed
vigilance
vivacious

wary
watchfulness
weariness
weary
woe
wonder
worried
wrathful

zeal
zest

JOURNAL IT OUT

What role did they play in your life?

_____
_____
_____
_____

How does the loss influence your life? (Mentally, physically, and spiritually)

_____
_____
_____
_____

When did you see them or talk to them most?

_____
_____
_____
_____

What memory keeps spinning in your head?

_____
_____
_____
_____

Are you feeling any regrets or remorse?

_____
_____
_____
_____

Does this loss bring up other compressed emotions or experiences?

_____
_____
_____
_____

JOURNAL IT OUT

How does this loss impact the people around you?

_____
_____
_____
_____

How are you taking the time to grieve?

_____
_____
_____
_____

Who is your support system through this time of loss?

_____
_____
_____
_____

What are ways you can take care of yourself?

_____
_____
_____
_____

Take the time to process memories, life events, and the stages of grief you feel as it comes. Don't put a timeline on your grief. Process the emotions.

_____
_____
_____
_____

STAGES OF GRIEF

DENIAL *(this can't be happening)*

Individuals may refuse to accept the fact that a loss has occurred. They may minimize or outright deny the situation. It is suggested that loved ones & professionals be forward & honest about losses to not prolong the denial stage.

ANGER *(why is this happening to me?)*

When an individual realizes that a loss has occurred, they may become angry at themselves or others. They may argue that the situation is unfair & try to place the blame.

BARGAINING *(I will do anything to change this)*

In bargaining, the individual may try to change or delay their loss. For example, they may try to convince a partner to return after a breakup, or search for unlikely cures in the case of a terminal illness.

DEPRESSION *(what's the point of going on after this loss?)*

At the stage of depression, the individual has come to recognize that a loss has occurred or will occur. The individual may isolate themselves & spend time crying & grieving. Depression is a precursor to acceptance because the individual has come to recognize their loss.

ACCEPTANCE *(it's going to be okay)*

Finally, the individual will come to accept their loss. They understand the situation logically, & they have come to terms emotionally with the situation.

MY STAGES OF GRIEF

Describe how each of these stages of grief has affected you.

DENIAL *(this can't be happening)*

ANGER *(why is this happening to me?)*

BARGAINING *(I will do anything to change this)*

DEPRESSION *(what's the point of going on after this loss?)*

ACCEPTANCE *(it's going to be okay)*

NORMAL VERSUS COMPLICATED GRIEF

Here are some typical signs and symptoms of what can be considered "normal grief," which may last days, weeks, or several months. Remember, there is no universal timeline for grief.

- Crying or sobbing
- Sleep disturbance – too much or too little
- Lack of energy
- Feeling apathetic or lethargic throughout the day
- Appetite changes – under or over eating
- Social withdrawal, including avoiding people or social events
- Trouble concentrating or focusing on tasks at work, home, school or elsewhere
- Confusion or questioning your spiritual or religious beliefs, general life goals, and choices Feeling angry, guilty, lonely, depressed, empty, sad, etc. but still capable of feeling happy or content.

Sometimes the intensity of grief does not dissipate and can develop into a serious psychological problem that can keep you from going about your daily activities or functioning adequately in your family or work life. Here are some symptoms of a more serious type of grief that may require professional help.

- Obsessing or ruminating constantly over your loss
- Feeling a deep, unbearable sadness that does not ease up
- Expressing a sense of doom, gloom, and despair about your life
- Being irritable and short-tempered
- Ongoing sleep problems
- Poor grooming and personal appearance (not caring about how you look)
- Refusing to or unable to leave your home
- Feeling angry and bitter toward the world
- Feeling guilty or self-blaming, thinking perhaps the death was your fault
- Difficulty trusting others, pushing others away
- Extended period of withdrawal from social interactions and previous activities
- Minimizing, denying, or getting defensive when asked about your grief
- Feeling distracted or disengaged at work, school, or home
- Numbness or detachment
- Escalation of preexisting psychological problems (e.g., depression, PTSD, anxiety disorder, substance abuse, etc.)
- Needing to be around mementos and reminders of your lost loved one, or, by contrast, strongly avoiding any reminders
- Trouble managing daily affairs or completing tasks
- Being reckless, impulsive, or potentially self-destructive
- Persistent wish that you had died along with your loved one
- Talk of suicide, or actual suicide attempts

If you have been suffering from these symptoms from more than 6 months, seek the help of a mental health professional, ideally one who specializes in grief, loss, bereavement, etc.

MY MOURNING RIGHTS

Grieving is a difficult process in any situation. As someone suffering from the loss of a loved one, you may feel as though you are not handling the situation like you should or would like to. While people are generally well meaning, you will often get loads of advice about how you "should" handle your own grief. Just remember, you have a right to your own feelings.

As someone grieving a profound loss, remember that you have the following rights when mourning your loved one:

- I have the right to grieve the death of my loved one.

- I have the right to grieve the death on my own time.

- I have the right to my feelings and upsurges of sorrow.

- I have the right to grieve even when others think I should be over it.

- I have the right to remember and talk about my lost loved one at any time.

- I have the right to demonstrate my feelings of grief in my own way.

- I have the right to repeat a stage of grieving as many times as I need to.

    - I have the right to phase in & out of a particular stage of grieving as often as I need to.

- I have the right to attach my own meanings to the loss.

    - I have the right to expect you to empathize with my grieving because some day you'll be in my place.

Other rights:
Is there anyone in my life who, though maybe well-intentioned, isn't respecting these rights of mine? If so, list them below and plan a time to talk to them. Bring this worksheet if it helps.

GRIEVING RITUALS

Sometimes it can be helpful to develop some personal rituals for people who are experiencing deep loss. Rituals that people found to be most helpful were not done in public or social settings. They were private and personal. This worksheet is designed to help you think about some personal rituals to help you through your grieving process. You may choose to do a ritual every day, or on the anniversary of your loss. It's entirely up to you.

Play music that reminds you of your loved one.
Watch a movie that reminds you of your loved one.
Write a letter to your loved one.
      Light a candle at special times of the day or week to remind you of your loved one.
Create a scrapbook of memories, letters, pictures, or other sentimental things.
Spend some times listening to your loved one's favorite music.
Plant a tree in memory of your loved one.
Make a donation to a cause that your loved one was passionate about.
Visit your loved one's burial site.
Carry something special that reminds you of your loved one.
Create a work of art that in memory of your loved one.
Prepare and eat a special meal in memory of your loved one.
Read aloud an inspirational poem or prayer.
Set a place at the table for your loved one.
Dedicate a song on the radio to your loved one.
Go on a walk and carry a picture of your loved one.

Other: _____

Other: _____

Other: _____

Other: _____

Write down dates and times when you think a personal ritual might be helpful for you.

Write down people who you might want to talk to about your rituals and your reactions.

Now record below how these rituals affected you. In the last column, rate each ritual on how successful it was in helping you feel more hopeful and in control of your feelings with a 1 being not helpful to a 10 being very helpful.

Date	Ritual Type	Immediate Emotional Reaction	Longer Term Emotional Reaction	Rating

GRIEF SENTENCE COMPLETION

Right now, I feel:

I feel the saddest when:

The thing I miss most about the person I lost:

Since the loss, things have been different because:

If I could ask the person I lost one question, I would ask:

My favorite memory with the person I lost:

One thing I learned from the person I lost:

EMOTIONAL NUMBING

What emotions do you not allow yourself to feel?

Why do you think it's easier to not feel? How did you learn to not feel?

What do you fear would happen if you felt sadness?

What do you fear would happen if you felt joy?

What do you fear would happen if you felt anger?

What emotions would you like to feel again?

How does being emotionally numb affect your relationships?

SAYING GOODBYE

I am saying goodbye because:

Saying goodbye makes me feel:

I remember a time when we:

You taught me:

Something I want you to know is:

I will always remember:

MY LETTER TO YOU

NOTES

NOTES

SELF CARE CHECKLIST

WEEK OF

	S	M	T	W	T	F	S

DAILY JOURNAL

Date:

Topic:

DAILY JOURNAL

Date:

Topic:

DAILY JOURNAL

Date:

Topic:

DAILY JOURNAL

Date:

Topic:

DAILY JOURNAL

Date:

Topic:

_____
_____
_____
_____
_____
_____
_____
_____
_____
_____
_____
_____
_____
_____

DAILY JOURNAL

Date:

Topic:

DAILY JOURNAL

Date:

Topic:

Now record below how these rituals affected you. In the last column, rate each ritual on how successful it was in helping you feel more hopeful and in control of your feelings with a 1 being not helpful to a 10 being very helpful.

Date	Ritual Type	Immediate Emotional Reaction	Longer Term Emotional Reaction	Rating

GRIEF SENTENCE COMPLETION

Right now, I feel:

I feel the saddest when:

The thing I miss most about the person I lost:

Since the loss, things have been different because:

If I could ask the person I lost one question, I would ask:

My favorite memory with the person I lost:

One thing I learned from the person I lost:

EMOTIONAL NUMBING

What emotions do you not allow yourself to feel?

Why do you think it's easier to not feel? How did you learn to not feel?

What do you fear would happen if you felt sadness?

What do you fear would happen if you felt joy?

What do you fear would happen if you felt anger?

What emotions would you like to feel again?

How does being emotionally numb affect your relationships?

SAYING GOODBYE

I am saying goodbye because:

Saying goodbye makes me feel:

I remember a time when we:

You taught me:

Something I want you to know is:

I will always remember:

MY LETTER TO YOU

NOTES

NOTES

SELF CARE CHECKLIST

WEEK OF

	S	M	T	W	T	F	S

DAILY JOURNAL

Date:

Topic:

DAILY JOURNAL

Date:

Topic:

DAILY JOURNAL

Date:

Topic:

DAILY JOURNAL

Date:

Topic:

DAILY JOURNAL

Date:

Topic:

DAILY JOURNAL

Date:

Topic:

DAILY JOURNAL

Date:

Topic:

Now record below how these rituals affected you. In the last column, rate each ritual on how successful it was in helping you feel more hopeful and in control of your feelings with a 1 being not helpful to a 10 being very helpful.

Date	Ritual Type	Immediate Emotional Reaction	Longer Term Emotional Reaction	Rating

GRIEF SENTENCE COMPLETION

Right now, I feel:

I feel the saddest when:

The thing I miss most about the person I lost:

Since the loss, things have been different because:

If I could ask the person I lost one question, I would ask:

My favorite memory with the person I lost:

One thing I learned from the person I lost:

EMOTIONAL NUMBING

What emotions do you not allow yourself to feel?

Why do you think it's easier to not feel? How did you learn to not feel?

What do you fear would happen if you felt sadness?

What do you fear would happen if you felt joy?

What do you fear would happen if you felt anger?

What emotions would you like to feel again?

How does being emotionally numb affect your relationships?

SAYING GOODBYE

I am saying goodbye because:

Saying goodbye makes me feel:

I remember a time when we:

You taught me:

Something I want you to know is:

I will always remember:

MY LETTER TO YOU

NOTES

NOTES

SELF CARE CHECKLIST

WEEK OF

	S	M	T	W	T	F	S

DAILY JOURNAL

Date:

Topic:

_____

_____

_____

_____

_____

_____

_____

_____

_____

_____

_____

_____

_____

DAILY JOURNAL

Date:

Topic:

DAILY JOURNAL

Date:

Topic:

DAILY JOURNAL

Date:

Topic:

DAILY JOURNAL

Date:

Topic:

DAILY JOURNAL

Date:

Topic:

DAILY JOURNAL

Date:

Topic:

Now record below how these rituals affected you. In the last column, rate each ritual on how successful it was in helping you feel more hopeful and in control of your feelings with a 1 being not helpful to a 10 being very helpful.

Date	Ritual Type	Immediate Emotional Reaction	Longer Term Emotional Reaction	Rating

GRIEF SENTENCE COMPLETION

Right now, I feel:

I feel the saddest when:

The thing I miss most about the person I lost:

Since the loss, things have been different because:

If I could ask the person I lost one question, I would ask:

My favorite memory with the person I lost:

One thing I learned from the person I lost:

EMOTIONAL NUMBING

What emotions do you not allow yourself to feel?

Why do you think it's easier to not feel? How did you learn to not feel?

What do you fear would happen if you felt sadness?

What do you fear would happen if you felt joy?

What do you fear would happen if you felt anger?

What emotions would you like to feel again?

How does being emotionally numb affect your relationships?

SAYING GOODBYE

I am saying goodbye because:

Saying goodbye makes me feel:

I remember a time when we:

You taught me:

Something I want you to know is:

I will always remember:

MY LETTER TO YOU

NOTES

NOTES

SELF CARE CHECKLIST

WEEK OF

	S	M	T	W	T	F	S

DAILY JOURNAL

Date:

Topic:

DAILY JOURNAL

Date:

Topic:

DAILY JOURNAL

Date:

Topic:

DAILY JOURNAL

Date:

Topic:

DAILY JOURNAL

Date:

Topic:

DAILY JOURNAL

Date:

Topic:

DAILY JOURNAL

Date:

Topic:

Now record below how these rituals affected you. In the last column, rate each ritual on how successful it was in helping you feel more hopeful and in control of your feelings with a 1 being not helpful to a 10 being very helpful.

Date	Ritual Type	Immediate Emotional Reaction	Longer Term Emotional Reaction	Rating

GRIEF SENTENCE COMPLETION

Right now, I feel:

I feel the saddest when:

The thing I miss most about the person I lost:

Since the loss, things have been different because:

If I could ask the person I lost one question, I would ask:

My favorite memory with the person I lost:

One thing I learned from the person I lost:

EMOTIONAL NUMBING

What emotions do you not allow yourself to feel?

Why do you think it's easier to not feel? How did you learn to not feel?

What do you fear would happen if you felt sadness?

What do you fear would happen if you felt joy?

What do you fear would happen if you felt anger?

What emotions would you like to feel again?

How does being emotionally numb affect your relationships?

SAYING GOODBYE

I am saying goodbye because:

Saying goodbye makes me feel:

I remember a time when we:

You taught me:

Something I want you to know is:

I will always remember:

MY LETTER TO YOU

NOTES

NOTES

SELF CARE CHECKLIST

WEEK OF

	S	M	T	W	T	F	S

DAILY JOURNAL

Date:

Topic:

DAILY JOURNAL

Date:

Topic:

DAILY JOURNAL

Date:

Topic:

DAILY JOURNAL

Date:

Topic:

DAILY JOURNAL

Date:

Topic:

———————————— DAILY JOURNAL ————————————

Date:

Topic:

DAILY JOURNAL

Date:

Topic:

Now record below how these rituals affected you. In the last column, rate each ritual on how successful it was in helping you feel more hopeful and in control of your feelings with a 1 being not helpful to a 10 being very helpful.

Date	Ritual Type	Immediate Emotional Reaction	Longer Term Emotional Reaction	Rating

GRIEF SENTENCE COMPLETION

Right now, I feel:

I feel the saddest when:

The thing I miss most about the person I lost:

Since the loss, things have been different because:

If I could ask the person I lost one question, I would ask:

My favorite memory with the person I lost:

One thing I learned from the person I lost:

EMOTIONAL NUMBING

What emotions do you not allow yourself to feel?

Why do you think it's easier to not feel? How did you learn to not feel?

What do you fear would happen if you felt sadness?

What do you fear would happen if you felt joy?

What do you fear would happen if you felt anger?

What emotions would you like to feel again?

How does being emotionally numb affect your relationships?

SAYING GOODBYE

I am saying goodbye because:

Saying goodbye makes me feel:

I remember a time when we:

You taught me:

Something I want you to know is:

I will always remember:

MY LETTER TO YOU

NOTES

NOTES

SELF CARE CHECKLIST

WEEK OF

	S	M	T	W	T	F	S

DAILY JOURNAL

Date:

Topic:

DAILY JOURNAL

Date:

Topic:

DAILY JOURNAL

Date:

Topic:

DAILY JOURNAL

Date:

Topic:

DAILY JOURNAL

Date:

Topic:

DAILY JOURNAL

Date:

Topic:

DAILY JOURNAL

Date:

Topic:

Now record below how these rituals affected you. In the last column, rate each ritual on how successful it was in helping you feel more hopeful and in control of your feelings with a 1 being not helpful to a 10 being very helpful.

Date	Ritual Type	Immediate Emotional Reaction	Longer Term Emotional Reaction	Rating

GRIEF SENTENCE COMPLETION

Right now, I feel:

I feel the saddest when:

The thing I miss most about the person I lost:

Since the loss, things have been different because:

If I could ask the person I lost one question, I would ask:

My favorite memory with the person I lost:

One thing I learned from the person I lost:

EMOTIONAL NUMBING

What emotions do you not allow yourself to feel?

Why do you think it's easier to not feel? How did you learn to not feel?

What do you fear would happen if you felt sadness?

What do you fear would happen if you felt joy?

What do you fear would happen if you felt anger?

What emotions would you like to feel again?

How does being emotionally numb affect your relationships?

SAYING GOODBYE

I am saying goodbye because:

Saying goodbye makes me feel:

I remember a time when we:

You taught me:

Something I want you to know is:

I will always remember:

MY LETTER TO YOU

NOTES

NOTES

SELF CARE CHECKLIST

WEEK OF

	S	M	T	W	T	F	S

DAILY JOURNAL

Date:

Topic:

DAILY JOURNAL

Date:

Topic:

DAILY JOURNAL

Date:

Topic:

DAILY JOURNAL

Date:

Topic:

DAILY JOURNAL

Date:

Topic:

DAILY JOURNAL

Date:

Topic:

DAILY JOURNAL

Date:

Topic:

Made in the USA
Las Vegas, NV
22 September 2023